The Ladies' Book of Baking

First published in 2013
LOVE FOOD is an imprint of Parragon Books Ltd

Parragon
Chartist House
15–17 Trim Street
Bath, BA1 1HA, UK

ISBN: 978-1-4723-1109-2

Printed in China

Project managed by **Annabel King**
Designed by **Lisa McCormick**
Cover illustration by **Catharine Collingridge** www.catharinecollingridge.co.uk
Photography by **Sian Irvine**
Introduction and additional text by **Anna-Marie Julyan**
New recipe text by **Christine McFadden**
Additional photography by **Henry Sparrow**

NOTES FOR THE READER

This book uses standard kitchen measuring spoons and cups. All spoon and cup measurements are level
unless otherwise indicated. Unless otherwise stated, milk is assumed to be whole, butter is assumed to be
salted, eggs are large, individual vegetables are medium, and pepper is freshly ground black pepper. Unless
otherwise stated, all root vegetables should be washed and peeled before using.

Garnishes and serving suggestions are all optional and not necessarily included in the recipe ingredients
or method. The times given are only an approximate guide. Preparation times differ according to the
techniques used by different people and the cooking times may also vary from those given. Optional
ingredients, variations, or serving suggestions have not been included in the calculations.

Recipes using raw or very lightly cooked eggs should be avoided by infants, the elderly, pregnant
women, and people with weakened immune systems. Pregnant and breast-feeding women are advised
to avoid eating peanuts and peanut products. People with nut allergies should be aware that some of
the prepared ingredients used in the recipes in this book may contain nuts. Always check the packaging
before use. Vegetarians should be aware that some of the prepared ingredients used in the recipes
in this book may contain animal products. Always check the package before use.

Introduction

Baking has officially come out of the closet, or, to be precise, the cupboard. Where once a passion for creating elegant petit fours was at best old-fashioned, the trend for home baking means we can once again make a song and dance in the kitchen, invite friends around, and, yes, even throw tea parties.

What a relief that there's no need to go on pretending, because the truth is that ladies love baking. The trend for cupcakes, muffins, whoopie pies, and tarts of every hue, flavor, and style has got us reaching for our pastry bags, scouring Web sites for vintage china, and coveting cake stands.

Where once ladies met for tea or coffee and enjoyed cake baked by a pro, modern ladies are the cooks. This gives us the added bonus of learning a lifelong talent for keeping loved ones in freshly baked pies. (Do not underestimate the benefits.)

With more than 50 recipes to choose from, *The Ladies' Book of Baking* is intended as a source of inspiration, both for the type of cake or pastry to serve and how to display the finished result. Beautiful baking doesn't finish in the kitchen. Matching your recipe to the occasion, serving it with a little flair and imagination, then watching people enjoy it is as important as mixing the ingredients in the first place.

A trend for miniature cakes demonstrates that these days we really do like to have our cake and eat it, too. Thinking practically, however, it provides a chance to experiment with flavors, finishing with some-thing that appears more intricate and complicated than it is.

Think of miniature mango cakes with a dusting of confectioners' sugar, classic yellow cake batter baked as miniature cupcakes, or small, caramelized apple tarts. Better than giant cookies or ten-tiered cakes, they provide a taste of heaven without blowing your sugar intake for the entire week on one treat.

What is it about this baking that makes it so popular? Ultimately, baking is comforting—from turning the much-thumbed pages of your favorite recipes to the warm smell of spiced apple pie cupcakes in the oven. If you're being thrifty, baking is a way of saving money, while increasingly people are realizing that home baking is not some kind of impossible task best approached with caution and a hotline to your nearest supermarket bakery. You can start with straightforward recipes and gradually build a repertoire.

A NOTE ON INGREDIENTS

Flour, essential to so much baking, is always best stored somewhere cool and dry. If you tend to bake in bursts with long, fallow periods in between, then remember to check the expiration date. Keep in mind that butter has a better flavor than vegetable shortening or margarine, but it will often need softening before you begin; the lowest setting on your microwave is handy if you forget to take it out in advance. Eggs should be used at room temperature and fruit is best unwaxed. You'll find that superfine sugar produces a smoother texture than granulated. If you don't have superfine sugar on hand, process the same quantity of granulated sugar in a food processor for a minute.

GENERAL TIPS

This book covers pastry, classic cakes, cookies, family-style baked goods, and ideas for different occasions. Of course, as you become familiar with a recipe, you might decide to adjust it, but as a general rule, it's a good idea to read a recipe all the way through first before you try it. Some cooks advise measuring out all the ingredients beforehand, but if that's not your thing, just make sure that you've read ahead, then start baking in your usual style. And let's face it: some cooks are simply messier than others. At least a smudge of frosting on your forehead shows you're not afraid to use some elbow grease.

It's always a good idea to start by preheating the oven and preparing whatever cake pan you are using before you begin. Unless you're chilling pastry or letting bread dough rise, don't leave doughs standing; get them in the oven to bake ASAP. Certainly when it comes to classic cakes and pastries, accuracy is important, but the more you bake, the more you'll learn where you can adjust a recipe.

If you're giving a party, or someone important is coming to dinner, it's probably worth baking a recipe you're familiar with and forgetting about that triple-layered chocolate confection shaped like a swan— for now, at least.

Once you've mastered the basics, you can start to think about the endless options for presentation. The trend for all things vintage is fantastic if your style is eclectic, as is a talent for collecting mismatched china. Save cookie tins at Christmas and look for items such as old hatboxes, which can be stacked to raise cakes to different levels, making them more eye-catching. It all depends on the occasion. Equally, you may want to stick with a more traditional style, using classic white linen on the table and dressing the table properly. A wealth of frosting and decorating paraphernalia available from specialty baking stores makes it much easier to decorate cakes without getting confectioners' sugar everywhere, letting you combine the best of traditional baking methods with modern bakeware and frosting gadgets. A little forward planning and a few simple techniques will have you turning out beautiful cakes that fit the occasion and impress every time, and make you proud to be hostess. Take your time, relax, and enjoy being a lady with absolutely no need for a professional cook, because it's actually much more fun doing it yourself.

Let *The Ladies' Book of Baking* be your gentle guide to turning out the most delicious pies, pastries, and cakes and presenting them in your own inimitable style. Whether you're catering for a party, baking for your family, or even just for yourself, follow the hints and tips in this book and you should create wonderful successes. Remember that your cakes will be individual because they were made by you. It's the love and care put into each batch that give the most joy to those who eat them—and to you, as the cook.

Afternoon Tea

Afternoon Tea

We have Anna, 7th Duchess of Bedford, to thank for coming up with the ritual of "afternoon tea" which is now popular around the globe. One afternoon in 1840 she rang her bell to request that a tray of tea, bread, butter, and cake be brought to her room. Unfortunately, times change; you can ring your bell as hard as you want, but a certain amount of forward planning, baking, and brewing is now required for the same result.

In our hectic modern world, treat this occasion as a valuable opportunity to stop the clock (somewhere between 4 and 5 p.m.), spend time with good friends and spread a little joy. Of course, just how you play it is a matter of personal preference. By the early twentieth century, afternoon tea was quite the social occasion in England, replete with intricate tea services and a system of anxiously meted out etiquette.

For an easy, modern-day take on afternoon tea follow a few simple rules. Arrange the cake stand with bite-size sandwiches on the bottom tier, scones in the middle, and delicate cakes on top. The hostess is in charge of pouring tea, unless there are more than a tableful of guests—in which case, nominate a couple of friends to help. Add milk to the poured tea and refrain from clinking the teaspoon noisily. Hold both cup and saucer unless seated. There is no need to stick one's pinkie in the air—and under absolutely no circumstance dunk cookies.

The "rules" are, of course, open to interpretation, because this is your event, but one piece of advice worth remembering is to plan ahead. This equipment list (right) is a good place to start.

Airtight tea caddy
Teapot
Urn or metal pitcher for hot water
Teacups and saucers
Dessert plates
Dessert forks
Butter knives
Teaspoons
Tea strainer and holder
Milk pitcher
Napkins (ideally linen)
Tablecloth
Sugar bowl with spoon or tongs
Cake stand
Cake plate
Tray

HOW TO MAKE THE PERFECT CUP OF TEA

Fill the kettle with freshly drawn water and just before it reaches boiling point, swirl some hot water in your teapot, then discard. Use one heaping teaspoon of tea leaves per person plus one for the pot. Pour boiling water over the leaves and let the tea steep for 3–6 minutes, depending on the size of tea leaves. Give the pot a good stir before pouring through a strainer into cups. Add cold, fresh milk to taste.

Mini Strawberry Sponge Cakes

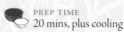 **MAKES**
12

 PREP TIME
20 mins, plus cooling

COOK TIME
15 mins

Ingredients

5 tablespoons salted butter, softened, plus extra for greasing

⅓ superfine sugar or granulated sugar

½ cup all-purpose flour

½ teaspoon baking powder

1 egg

1 egg yolk

1 teaspoon vanilla extract

DECORATION

⅔ heavy cream

⅓ strawberry jam or preserves

⅔ cup confectioners' sugar

1 tablespoon lemon juice

Method

1 Preheat the oven to 350°F. Grease and line the bottoms of a 12-cup cupcake pan. Put the butter, superfine sugar, flour, baking powder, egg, egg yolk, and vanilla in a mixing bowl and beat together with an electric handheld mixer until it is smooth and creamy.

2 Using a teaspoon, spoon the batter into the cups and level with the back of the spoon. Bake in the preheated oven for 15 minutes, or until risen and just firm to the touch. Let stand in the pan for 5 minutes, then transfer to a wire rack to cool.

3 For the decoration, whip the cream until it just peaks. Slice the cakes in half horizontally, using a small serrated knife. Press 2 tablespoons of the jam through a small strainer into a bowl to extract the seeds. Put the strained jam in a small paper pastry bag and snip off the tip. Sandwich the cakes together with the remaining jam and cream.

4 Beat the confectioners' sugar and lemon juice together in a bowl until smooth. Spoon the icing over the cakes, spreading it just to the edges. Pipe dots of jam on top of each cake and draw a toothpick through them.

3

3

4

Frosted Carrot Cake

SERVES
16

PREP TIME
20 mins, plus cooling

COOK TIME
40–45 mins

Ingredients

¾ cup sunflower oil, plus extra for greasing

¾ cup firmly packed light brown sugar

3 eggs, beaten

3 carrots, shredded

½ cup golden raisins

½ cup walnut pieces

grated rind of 1 orange

1⅓ cups all-purpose flour

1¼ teaspoons baking powder

1 teaspoon baking soda

1 teaspoon ground cinnamon

½ teaspoon grated nutmeg

strips of orange zest, to decorate

FROSTING

1 cup cream cheese

¾ cup confectioners' sugar

2 teaspoons orange juice

Method

1 Preheat the oven to 350°F. Grease and line the bottom of a 9-inch square cake pan.

2 In a large bowl, beat together the oil, brown sugar, and eggs. Stir in the shredded carrots, golden raisins, walnuts, and orange rind.

3 Sift together the flour, baking powder, baking soda, cinnamon, and nutmeg, then stir into the carrot mixture.

4 Spoon the batter into the prepared cake pan and bake in the preheated oven for 40–45 minutes, until well-risen and firm to the touch.

5 Remove the cake from the oven and set on a wire rack for 5 minutes. Turn out onto the wire rack to cool completely.

6 For the frosting, combine the cream cheese, confectioners' sugar, and orange juice in a bowl and beat until smooth. Spread over the top of the cake and swirl with a spatula. Decorate with strips of orange zest and serve cut into squares.

2

4

6

Rich Fruitcake

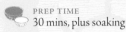

SERVES
16

PREP TIME
30 mins, plus soaking

COOK TIME
2¼–2¾ hrs

Ingredients

2⅓ cups golden raisins

1½ cups raisins

1 cup chopped dried apricots

⅔ cup chopped, pitted dates

¼ cup dark rum or brandy (optional)

finely grated rind and juice of 1 orange

2 sticks unsalted butter, softened, plus extra for greasing

1 cup firmly packed light brown sugar

4 eggs, beaten

⅓ cup chopped candied peel

½ cup quartered candied cherries

⅓ cup chopped crystallized ginger or preserved ginger

⅓ cup blanched almonds, chopped

1⅔ cups all-purpose flour

1 teaspoon ground allspice

Method

1 Put the golden raisins, raisins, apricots, and dates in a large bowl and stir in the rum, if using, orange rind, and orange juice. Cover and let soak for several hours or overnight.

2 Preheat the oven to 300°F. Grease an 8-inch round cake pan and line it with parchment paper.

3 Beat the butter and sugar together until pale and creamy. Gradually

beat in the eggs, beating hard after each addition. Stir in the soaked fruits, candied peel, candied cherries, crystallized ginger, and almonds.

4 Sift the flour and allpice, then fold them lightly and evenly into the mixture. Spoon the batter into the prepared cake pan and smooth the surface, making a slight depression in the center with the back of the spoon.

5 Bake in the preheated oven for 2¼–2¾ hours, or until the cake is beginning to shrink away from the sides and a toothpick inserted into the center comes out clean. Cool completely in the pan.

6 Turn out the cake and remove the parchment paper. Wrap in some wax paper and aluminum foil, then store for at least two months before use.

1

3

3

Lemon Drizzle Cake

🧁 **SERVES**
12

🫕 **PREP TIME**
20 mins, plus cooling

🧤 **COOK TIME**
1 hour

Ingredients

2 eggs

¾ cup superfine sugar or granulated sugar

¾ cup soft margarine, plus extra for greasing

finely grated rind of 1 lemon

1⅓ cups all-purpose flour

1¼ teaspoons baking powder

½ cup milk

confectioners' sugar, for dusting

SYRUP

1¼ cups confectioners' sugar

¼ cup fresh lemon juice

Method

1 Preheat the oven to 350°F. Grease a 7-inch square cake pan and line with parchment paper.

2 Put the eggs, superfine sugar, and margarine in a mixing bowl and beat well until smooth and fluffy. Stir in the lemon rind, then fold in the flour and baking powder lightly and evenly. Stir in the milk, mixing evenly, then spoon the batter into the prepared cake pan and smooth out the top.

3 Bake in the preheated oven for 45–50 minutes, or until golden brown and firm to the touch. Remove from the oven and stand the cake pan on a wire rack.

4 To make the syrup, put the confectioners' sugar and lemon juice in a small saucepan and heat gently, stirring until the sugar dissolves. Do not boil.

5 Prick the warm cake all over with a toothpick, and spoon the hot syrup evenly over the top, allowing it to be absorbed.

6 Let cool completely in the cake pan, then turn out the cake, cut into 12 pieces, and dust with a little confectioners' sugar before serving.

Cherry & Almond Loaves

MAKES
12

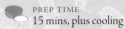
PREP TIME
15 mins, plus cooling

COOK TIME
25 mins

Ingredients

6 tablespoons salted butter, softened, plus extra for greasing

⅓ cup superfine sugar or granulated sugar

1 egg

1 egg yolk

½ cup all-purpose flour

½ teaspoon baking powder

½ teaspoon almond extract

½ cup ground almonds (almond meal)

¼ cup candied cherries

2 tablespoons slivered almonds

½ cup confectioners' sugar

2 teaspoons lemon juice

Method

1 Preheat the oven to 350°F. Grease and line the bottoms of 12 mini loaf pans with parchment paper. Put the butter, superfine sugar, egg, egg yolk, flour, baking powder, almond extract, and ground almonds in a mixing bowl and beat together with an electric handheld mixer until smooth and creamy. Chop the cherries and stir in.

2 Using a teaspoon, spoon the batter into the loaf pans and level with the back of the spoon. Break up the slivered almonds slightly by squeezing them in your hands and sprinkle them over the cake batter. Bake in the preheated oven for 25 minutes, or until risen and just firm to the touch. Let stand in the pans for 5 minutes, then transfer to a wire rack to cool.

3 Beat the confectioners' sugar and lemon juice together in a small bowl and drizzle over the cakes with a teaspoon. Let set.

20

Mango Cakes

 MAKES
12

PREP TIME
15 mins, plus soaking

COOK TIME
25 mins

Ingredients

½ cup finely chopped
dried mango

finely grated rind of 1 orange,
plus 3 tablespoons juice

⅓ cup shredded fresh coconut

6 tablespoons salted butter,
softened, plus extra for greasing

⅓ cup superfine sugar or
granulated sugar

1 egg

¾ cup all-purpose flour

¾ teaspoon baking power

confectioners' sugar, for dusting

Method

1 Preheat the oven to 350°F. Grease and
line the bottoms 12 mini loaf pans
with parchment paper. Put the mango
and orange juice in a small bowl and
let stand, covered, for 2–3 hours,
or until the orange juice is mostly
absorbed.

2 Put the coconut, butter, sugar, egg,
flour, baking powder, and orange rind
in a mixing bowl and beat together
with an electric handheld mixer until
smooth and pale. Stir in the mango
and any unabsorbed orange juice.

3 Using a teaspoon, spoon the batter
into the loaf pans and level with the
back of the spoon. Bake in the

preheated oven for 25 minutes, or
until risen and just firm to the touch.
Let stand in the pans for 5 minutes,
then transfer to a wire rack to cool.

4 Serve lightly dusted with
confectioners' sugar.

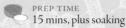

Scones

 MAKES
12

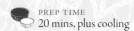 **PREP TIME**
20 mins, plus cooling

 COOK TIME
10–12 mins

Ingredients

3⅔ cups all-purpose flour, plus extra for dusting

½ teaspoon salt

2 teaspoons baking powder

4 tablespoons butter

2 tablespoons superfine sugar or granulated sugar

1 cup milk

3 tablespoons milk, for glazing

strawberry jam or preserves and thick whipped cream, to serve

Method

1 Preheat the oven to 425°F. Lightly flour or line a baking sheet with parchment paper.

2 Sift the flour, salt, and baking powder into a bowl. Rub in the butter until the mixture resembles bread crumbs. Stir in the sugar. Make a well in the center and pour in the milk. Stir in using a blunt knife and make a soft dough.

3 Turn the dough onto a floured surface and lightly flatten the dough until it is of an even thickness, about ½ inch. Don't be heavy-handed—scones need a light touch.

4 Use a 2½-inch pastry cutter to cut out the scones and place on the prepared baking sheet. Glaze with a little milk and bake in the preheated oven for 10–12 minutes, until golden and well risen. Cool on a wire rack and serve freshly baked, with strawberry jam and thick whipped cream.

2

2

4

The Afternoon Tea Party

You don't have to be extravagant to have an afternoon "tea party." Mismatched china creates a beautiful, vintage effect and it's fun hunting for pieces in flea markets and thrift shops. Save pretty jars to fill with flowers, decant loose tea into containers, and provide little finger bowls with slices of lemon and flower petals for your guests. Remember to arrange forks on the left, spoons and knives on the right. Why not follow a theme? A bridal shower, for example, can feature delicate macarons, champagne cocktails, and a fragrant variety of tea. Or you can do something as simple as drawing the curtains, lighting a fire in the fireplace, and having toast with butter and jelly in winter. Or arrange a vase of garden flowers on a lace tablecloth in the peak of summer to serve an English-style afternoon tea with scones, dishes of thick whipped cream, and strawberry jam or preserves.

Tea Rolls

🧺 MAKES
10–12

🥣 PREP TIME
25 mins, plus resting

🧤 COOK TIME
18–20 mins

Ingredients

1¼ cups milk

4 teaspoons dry yeast

¼ cup superfine sugar or granulated sugar

3⅓ cups white bread flour, plus extra for dusting

1 teaspoon salt

1 teaspoon ground allspice

¾ cup dried currants

2 tablespoons chopped candied peel

4 tablespoons butter, melted, plus extra for greasing

1 egg, beaten

sugar glaze made from 2 tablespoons sugar and 2 tablespoons warm milk

Method

1 Warm the milk in a saucepan until just lukewarm and add the yeast with 1 teaspoon of the sugar. Mix well and let froth in a warm place for 15 minutes.

2 Sift the flour, salt, and allspice into a large mixing bowl and add the currants, peel, and the remaining sugar. Make a well in the center of the dry ingredients and pour in the milk mixture, the melted butter, and egg.

Mix well using a wooden spoon at first and then by hand. Turn out onto a lightly floured surface and knead lightly until the dough is smooth and elastic.

3 Put the dough back into the bowl, cover with plastic wrap and let rise in a warm place for 40–45 minutes, until it has doubled in size. Knead the dough again lightly and divide into 10–12 even, round rolls, shaping well.

4 Preheat the oven to 425°F. Place the rolls on two greased baking sheets, cover with a damp dish towel, and let rise again for 30–40 minutes. Bake the tea rolls in the oven for 18–20 minutes, until they are golden brown. Remove from the oven, place on a wire rack, and glaze with the sugar glaze while still hot.

2

3

4

Vanilla Macarons

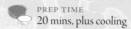

MAKES
16

PREP TIME
20 mins, plus cooling

COOK TIME
10–15 mins

Ingredients

¾ cup ground almonds
(almond meal)

1 cup confectioners' sugar

2 extra-large egg whites

¼ cup superfine sugar

½ teaspoon vanilla extract

FILLING

4 tablespoons unsalted butter,
softened

½ teaspoon vanilla extract

1 cup confectioners' sugar, sifted

Method

1 Put the ground almonds and confectioners' sugar in a food processor and process for 15 seconds. Sift the mixture into a bowl. Line two baking sheets with parchment paper.

2 Put the egg whites in a clean, grease-free bowl and beat until holding soft peaks. Gradually beat in the superfine sugar to make a firm, glossy meringue. Beat in the vanilla extract.

3 Using a spatula, fold the almond mixture into the meringue, one-third at a time. When all the dry ingredients are thoroughly incorporated, continue to cut and fold the mixture until it forms a shiny batter.

4 Pour the batter into a pastry bag fitted with a ½-inch plain tip. Pipe 32 small circles onto the prepared baking sheets. Tap the baking sheets firmly onto a work surface to remove air bubbles. Let stand at room temperature for 30 minutes. Preheat the oven to 325°F.

5 Bake in the preheated oven for 10–15 minutes. Cool for 10 minutes, then carefully peel the macarons off the parchment paper. Let cool completely.

6 To make the filling, beat the butter and vanilla extract in a bowl until pale and fluffy. Gradually beat in the confectioners' sugar until smooth and creamy. Use to sandwich together pairs of macarons.

Cream Palmiers

 MAKES
8

 PREP TIME
20 mins, plus cooling

COOK TIME
18–20 mins

Ingredients

3 tablespoons granulated sugar

1 sheet ready-to-bake puff pastry

1¾ cups heavy whipping cream

1 tablespoon confectioners'
sugar, sifted

few drops vanilla extract

2 tablespoons strawberry jam
or preserves

Method

1 Preheat the oven to 425°F. Dust the work surface with half the sugar and roll the pastry out on the sugared work surface to 10 x 12 inches.

2 Sprinkle the rest of the sugar over the pastry and gently roll over it with the rolling pin. Roll the two short sides of the pastry into the center until they

meet, moisten the edges that meet with a little water, and press together gently. Cut across the roll into 16 even slices.

3 Place the slices, cut-side down, on a dampened baking sheet. Use a rolling pin to flatten each one slightly.

4 Bake in the preheated oven for 15–18 minutes, until crisp and golden brown, turning the palmiers over halfway through cooking. Transfer to a wire rack to cool.

5 Whip the cream, confectioners' sugar, and vanilla extract until softly peaking. Sandwich together the palmiers with the jam and whipped cream.

Madeleines

 MAKES
30

 PREP TIME
15 mins

 COOK TIME
8–10 mins

Ingredients

3 eggs

1 egg yolk

1 teaspoon vanilla extract

¾ cup superfine sugar or
granulated sugar

1¼ cups all-purpose flour

1 teaspoon baking powder

1¼ sticks unsalted butter,
melted and cooled, plus extra
for greasing

Method

1 Preheat the oven to 375°F. Lightly
grease 30 cups in two to three
standard madeleine pans.

2 Put the eggs, egg yolk, vanilla extract,
and sugar in a large bowl and beat
with an electric handheld mixer until
pale and thick.

3 Sift in the flour and baking powder
and fold in lightly and evenly, using
a metal spoon. Fold in the melted
butter evenly.

4 Spoon the batter into the prepared
pans, filling to about three-quarters
full. Bake in the preheated oven for
8–10 minutes, until risen and golden.

5 Remove the cakes carefully from the
pans and cool on a wire rack. They are
best served the day they are made.

Family Favorites

Family Favorites

There's nothing like the smell of a gorgeous cake baking in the oven to make you feel at home. While store-bought cakes are perfectly proportioned and immaculately presented, nothing can compare to a slice of homemade cake served fresh from the oven.

From a classic chocolate cake to warm spiced apple-pie cupcakes, the recipes in this chapter all have an ability to soothe and satisfy in quantities large enough to meet the demands of family life.

Get children involved with the simpler recipes and plan ahead by baking in batches and freezing as soon as the cakes have cooled in order to maintain maximum freshness.

Preheat your oven and measure your ingredients in advance to get the best results. There are also a few keys items to invest in, but it isn't necessary to buy everything at once; read the recipe before you start to be sure you have the basics. Other things you might find useful are listed in the box to the right.

Two shallow cake pans,
8–9 inches

Deep square cake pan, 7 inches

Tube pan, 9½ inches

12-cup muffin pan and cupcake pan

Muffin cups and cupcake paper liners

Paper cupcake liners

Large mixing bowl

Large metal spoon

Wire rack

Small and large spatulas

Sifter or fine-mesh strainer

Electric handheld mixer

Large pastry bag and large star tip

FOLLOW THE TIPS BELOW
TO GET PERFECT RESULTS

Eggs should be at room temperature. Always beat first and then gradually add them to the creamed mixture. Beat well after each addition to avoid curdling.

As soon as you introduce air into cake batter, whether in the form of sifted flour or beatened egg white, it is best to work gently, preserving as much air as possible. For best results, use a large metal spoon.

Bake in the center of the oven and don't be tempted to open the door too early—this can cause the cake to sink. To check if a sponge cake is ready, gently press the surface with your fingertips; it should be springy to the touch and not leave an impression. For deeper cakes, insert a toothpick into the center of the cake and it should come out clean.

Coffee & Walnut Cake

 SERVES
8

 PREP TIME
30 mins, plus cooling

 COOK TIME
20–25 mins

Ingredients

1½ sticks unsalted butter, softened, plus extra for greasing

¾ cup firmly packed light brown sugar

3 extra-large eggs, beaten

3 tablespoons strong black coffee

1⅓ cups all-purpose flour

1 tablespoon baking powder

1 cup walnut pieces

walnut halves, to decorate

FROSTING

1 stick unsalted butter, softened

1⅓ cups confectioners' sugar

1 tablespoon strong black coffee

½ teaspoon vanilla extract

Method

1 Preheat the oven to 350°F. Grease two 8-inch cake pans and line with parchment paper.

2 Beat together the butter and brown sugar until pale and creamy. Gradually add the eggs, beating well after each addition. Beat in the coffee.

3 Sift the flour and baking powder into the mixture, then fold in lightly and evenly with a metal spoon. Fold in the walnut pieces. Divide the batter between the prepared cake pans and smooth the surfaces. Bake in the preheated oven for 20–25 minutes, or until golden brown and springy to the touch. Turn out onto a wire rack to cool completely.

4 To make the frosting, beat together the butter, confectioners' sugar, coffee, and vanilla extract, mixing until smooth and creamy.

5 Use about half the frosting to sandwich the cakes together, then spread the remainder on top and swirl with a spatula. Decorate with walnut halves.

2

4

5

Red Velvet Cake

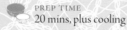

🍮 SERVES	🫙 PREP TIME	🧤 COOK TIME
12	20 mins, plus cooling	25–30 mins

Ingredients

2 sticks unsalted butter, plus extra for greasing

¼ cup water

⅔ cup unsweetened cocoa powder

3 eggs, beaten

1 cup buttermilk

2 teaspoons vanilla extract

2 tablespoons red edible food coloring

2 cups all-purpose flour

½ cup cornstarch

1½ teaspoons baking powder

1⅓ cups granulated sugar

FROSTING

1 cup cream cheese

3 tablespoons unsalted butter

3 tablespoons granulated sugar

1 teaspoon vanilla extract

Method

1 Preheat the oven to 375°F. Grease two 9-inch cake pans and line with parchment paper.

2 Put the butter, water, and cocoa powder in a small saucepan and heat gently, without boiling, stirring until melted and smooth. Remove from the heat and let cool slightly.

3 Beat together the eggs, buttermilk, vanilla extract, and food coloring in a bowl. Beat in the butter mixture. Sift together the flour, cornstarch, and baking powder, then stir into the mixture with the sugar.

4 Divide the batter between the prepared pans and bake in the preheated oven for 25–30 minutes, or

until risen and firm to the touch. Let cool in the pans for 3–4 minutes, then turn out onto a wire rack to cool completely.

5 To make the frosting, beat together all the ingredients until smooth. Use about half of the frosting to sandwich the cakes together, then spread the remainder over the top.

Pineapple & Coconut Cake

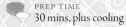

SERVES
12

PREP TIME
30 mins, plus cooling

COOK TIME
25 mins

Ingredients

1 (15½-ounce) can
pineapple slices, drained

1 stick unsalted butter, softened,
plus extra for greasing

¾ cup superfine sugar
or granulated sugar

2 eggs and 1 egg yolk, beaten

1¾ cups all-purpose flour, plus
extra for dusting

1 teaspoon baking powder

½ teaspoon baking soda

½ cup dried flaked coconut

FROSTING

¾ cup cream cheese

1⅓ cups confectioners' sugar

Method

1 Preheat the oven to 350°F. Grease
and lightly flour a 9½-inch tube pan.
Put the pineapple slices in a blender
or food processor and process briefly
until just crushed.

2 Beat together the butter and superfine
sugar until light and fluffy. Gradually
beat in the eggs until combined. Sift
together the flour, baking powder,
and baking soda over the egg mixture
and fold in. Then fold in the crushed
pineapple and the coconut.

3 Spoon the batter into the prepared
pan and bake in the preheated
oven for 25 minutes, or until a
toothpick inserted into the center
comes out clean.

4 Let cool in the pan for 10 minutes
before turning out onto a wire rack to
cool completely. To make the frosting,
mix together the cream cheese and
confectioners' sugar and spread over
the cooled cake.

Classic Chocolate Cake

SERVES
10

PREP TIME
40 mins, plus chilling

COOK TIME
25–30 mins

Ingredients

⅔ cup unsweetened cocoa powder

½ cup boiling water

1¾ sticks butter, softened, plus extra for greasing

⅔ cup superfine sugar or granulated sugar

⅓ cup firmly packed light brown sugar

4 eggs, beaten

1 teaspoon vanilla extract

1⅓ cups all-purpose flour

1½ teaspoons baking powder

FROSTING

8 ounces semisweet chocolate, broken into pieces

1 stick unsalted butter

½ cup heavy cream

Method

1 Preheat the oven to 350°F. Grease two 8-inch cake pans and line with parchment paper.

2 Blend the cocoa powder and water to a smooth paste and set aside. Put the butter, superfine sugar, and brown sugar into a large bowl and beat together until pale and creamy. Gradually beat in the eggs, then stir in the cocoa paste and vanilla extract.

3 Sift in the flour and baking powder and fold in gently. Divide the batter between the prepared pans. Bake in the preheated oven for 25–30 minutes, or until risen and just springy to the touch. Let cool in the pans for 5 minutes, then turn out onto a wire rack to cool completely.

4 To make the frosting, put the chocolate and butter into a heatproof bowl set over a saucepan of simmering water, making sure the bowl doesn't come in contact with the water, and heat until melted. Remove from the heat and stir in the cream. Let cool for 20 minutes, then chill in the refrigerator for 40–50 minutes, stirring occasionally, until thick enough to spread. Sandwich together the sponges with one-third of the frosting, then spread the remainder over the top of the cake.

2

3

4

Vanilla Frosted Cupcakes

MAKES
12

PREP TIME
15 mins, plus cooling

COOK TIME
15–20 mins

Ingredients

1 stick unsalted butter, softened

⅔ cup superfine sugar or granulated sugar

2 eggs, lightly beaten

1 cup all-purpose flour

1 teaspoon baking powder

1 tablespoon milk

crystallized rose petals, to decorate

FROSTING

1½ sticks unsalted butter, softened

2 teaspoons vanilla extract

2 tablespoons milk

2⅓ cups confectioners' sugar, sifted

Method

1 Preheat the oven to 350°F. Line a 12-cup cupcake pan with paper liners.

2 Put the butter and sugar in a bowl and beat together until light and fluffy. Gradually beat in the eggs. Sift in the flour and baking powder and fold in gently, using a metal spoon. Gently mix in the milk.

3 Spoon the batter into the paper liners. Bake in the preheated oven for 15–20 minutes, until golden brown and firm to the touch. Transfer to a cooling rack and let cool.

4 To make the frosting, put the butter, vanilla extract, and milk in a large bowl. Using an electric handheld mixer, beat the mixture until smooth. Gradually beat in the confectioners' sugar and continue beating for 2–3 minutes, until the frosting is light and creamy.

5 Spoon the frosting into a large pastry bag fitted with a large star tip and pipe swirls of the frosting onto the top of each cupcake. Decorate each cupcake with crystallized rose petals.

2

2

4

Molten Chocolate Cupcakes

 MAKES
9

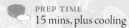 PREP TIME
15 mins, plus cooling

 COOK TIME
20 mins

Ingredients

¾ cup soft margarine

¾ cup superfine sugar or
granulated sugar

3 extra-large eggs

2 cups all-purpose flour

2 teaspoons baking powder

3 tablespoons cocoa powder

9 squares semisweet chocolate

confectioners' sugar, for dusting

Method

1 Preheat the oven to 375°F. Put nine
paper liners in two muffin pans.

2 Put the margarine, superfine sugar,
eggs, flour, baking powder, and cocoa
powder in a large bowl and, using an
electric handheld mixer, beat together
until just smooth.

3 Spoon half of the batter into the
paper liners. Using a teaspoon, make
an indentation in the center of each
cake. Break up the chocolate squares
and place a square on top of each
indentation, then spoon the remaining
cake batter on top.

4 Bake the cupcakes in the preheated
oven for 20 minutes, or until well
risen and springy to the touch. Let the
cupcakes cool for 2–3 minutes before
serving warm, dusted with sifted
confectioners' sugar.

1

2

3

The Perfect Presentation

When you've put time into baking delicious cakes and treats for a family get-together it's always worthwhile thinking about the presentation. A beautiful ceramic cake stand is a good investment. Use it for large family cakes, such as the Rich Fruitcake or Coffee & Walnut Cake, and it instantly adds elegance. It can also be used for miniature cakes or cupcakes. Make sure that you don't position the cakes too close together, or when one is removed, the others could be damaged or fall off.

Alternatively, for cupcakes, use a cupcake stand. These are available in kitchen supply stores and are ideal for displaying and serving a lot of cupcakes. Also available are disposable cardboard stands; these come in a variety of colors and patterns and are often a cheaper solution. In addition, think about pretty plates for people to put their cakes on and colorful paper napkins.

You can also add cake flags to your cakes and other baked goods to highlight the occasion or indicate the flavor. You can buy these premade, often themed for seasonal events, or make your own. To make your own, photocopy the designs on the opposite page or cut out a small piece of thin cardstock or paper, and use them as a template. Fold around a toothpick and glue the two halves together. For the heart-shaped ones, cut two identical shapes and glue them back-to-back on a toothpick. Try using different colors and patterns to match your theme.

Congratulations

Congratulations

EAT ME!

EAT ME!

Warm Spiced Apple Pie Cupcakes

MAKES
12

PREP TIME
20 mins, plus cooling

COOK TIME
30 mins

Ingredients

4 tablespoons butter, softened

⅓ cup raw brown sugar

1 egg, lightly beaten

15¼ cups all-purpose flour

1½ teaspoons baking powder

½ teaspoon ground allspice

1 large Granny Smith apple, peeled, cored, and finely chopped

1 tablespoon orange juice

TOPPING

⅓ cup all-purpose flour

½ teaspoon ground allspice

2 tablespoons butter

3 tablespoons granulated sugar

Method

1 Preheat the oven to 350°F. Line a 12-cup cupcake pan with 12 paper liners.

2 To make the topping, put the flour, allspice, butter, and sugar in a large bowl and rub in with your fingertips until the mixture resembles fine bread crumbs. Set aside.

3 To make the cupcakes, put the butter and sugar in a large bowl and beat together until light and fluffy, then gradually beat in the egg. Sift in the flour, baking powder, and allspice and fold into the mixture, then fold in the chopped apple and orange juice. Spoon the batter into the paper liners. Add the topping to cover the top of each cupcake and press down gently.

4 Bake in the preheated oven for 30 minutes, or until golden brown. Let the cupcakes cool in the pan for 2–3 minutes and serve warm, or let cool for 10 minutes and then transfer to a wire rack to cool completely.

Mini Chocolate Muffins

 MAKES
12

 PREP TIME
15 mins, plus cooling

COOK TIME
25 mins

Ingredients

3 tablespoons unsweetened
cocoa powder

½ cup all-purpose flour

¾ teaspoon baking powder

2 tablespoons light brown sugar

3 ounces milk chocolate,
coarsely chopped

1 egg

3 tablespoons milk

3 tablespoons salted butter, melted

2 ounces semisweet chocolate,
coarsely chopped

Method

1 Preheat the oven to 375°F. Line a minature 12-cup cupcake pan with 1¼-inch paper liners.

2 Sift the cocoa powder, flour, and baking powder into a mixing bowl. Stir in the light brown sugar and milk chocolate. In a separate mixing bowl, beat together the egg, milk, and butter with a fork until they are

evenly combined. Transfer the egg mixture into the flour. Gently fold the ingredients together until just mixed.

3 Spoon the batter into the paper liners. Bake in the preheated oven for 15 minutes, or until risen and just firm to the touch. Let the muffins stand in the tin for 2 minutes, then transfer them in their liners to a wire rack to cool.

4 Put the semisweet chocolate in a heatproof bowl set over a saucepan of simmering water, making sure the bowl doesn't come in contact with the water, and heat until melted. Using a teaspoon, drizzle the melted chocolate over the muffins and serve.

Raspberry Crumb Muffins

 MAKES
12

 PREP TIME
25 mins, plus cooling

COOK TIME
20 mins

Ingredients

2¼ cups all-purpose flour

1 tablespoon baking powder

½ teaspoon baking soda

pinch of salt

½ cup superfine sugar or
granulated sugar

2 eggs

1 cup plain yogurt

6 tablespoons butter, melted
and cooled

1 teaspoon vanilla extract

1 cup frozen raspberries

CRUMB TOPPING

⅓ cup all-purpose flour

1½ tablespoons butter

2 tablespoons granulated sugar

Method

1 Preheat the oven to 400°F. Line a 12-cup muffin pan with muffin cups.

2 To make the crumb topping, sift the flour into a bowl. Cut the butter into small pieces, add to the bowl with the flour, and rub it in with your fingertips until the mixture resembles fine bread crumbs. Stir in the sugar and set aside.

3 To make the muffins, sift together the flour, baking powder, baking soda, and salt into a large bowl. Stir in the sugar.

4 Lightly beat the eggs in a large bowl, then beat in the yogurt, butter, and vanilla extract. Make a well in the center of the dry ingredients, pour in the beaten liquid ingredients, and add the raspberries. Stir gently until just combined; do not overmix.

5 Spoon the batter into the prepared muffin pan. Sprinkle the crumb topping over each muffin and press down lightly. Bake in the preheated oven for about 20 minutes, until well risen, golden brown, and firm to the touch.

6 Let the muffins stand in the pan to cool for 5 minutes, then serve warm or transfer to a wire rack and let cool.

Pear & Chocolate Squares

MAKES
16

PREP TIME
20 mins, plus cooling

COOK TIME
1 hour 20 mins

Ingredients

1¼ cups whole-wheat flour

1¼ cups all-purpose white flour

1¼ teaspoons baking powder

1½ sticks butter, diced, plus extra for greasing

1 cup ground almonds (almond meal)

⅓ cup superfine sugar or granulated sugar

2 large, ripe Bosc pears, peeled, cored, and coarsely chopped

2 extra-large eggs, separated

⅓ cup unsweetened cocoa powder

2 teaspoons baking powder

¾ cup firmly packed dark brown sugar

⅓ cup milk

Method

1 Preheat the oven to 350°F. Grease and line the bottom of a deep 7-inch square cake pan. Sift the whole-wheat flour, all-purpose flour, and baking powder into a bowl. Add the butter and rub in with your fingertips until the mixture resembles fine bread crumbs.

2 Transfer about one-twelfth of the mixture to a separate bowl. Add the ground almonds, superfine sugar, pears, and the white of one egg to the remaining mixture. Mix well.

3 Sift together the cocoa powder and baking powder. Stir into the remaining butter mixture with the brown sugar. Add the egg white, remaining egg yolks, and milk. Mix well.

4 Spread half the chocolate batter over the bottom of the prepared cake pan. Spread the pear batter over the top. Cover with the remaining chocolate batter and smooth the surface. Bake in the preheated oven for 1 hour, 10 minutes–1 hour, 20 minutes, or until risen and the center is firm to the touch. Let cool in the pan, then turn out and cut into 16 squares.

1

3

4

Chocolate Brownies

MAKES
25

PREP TIME
15 mins, plus cooling

COOK TIME
18–20 mins

Ingredients

1 stick lightly salted butter, cut into pieces, plus extra for greasing

4 ounces semisweet chocolate, coarsely chopped

2 eggs

¾ cup firmly packed light brown sugar

2 teaspoons vanilla extract

½ cup all-purpose flour

¼ cup unsweetened cocoa powder

⅓ cup coarsely chopped pecans or walnuts

Method

1 Preheat the oven to 400°F. Grease and line a shallow 7-inch square cake pan.

2 Put the butter and chocolate in a heatproof bowl, set the bowl over a saucepan of gently simmering water, and heat until melted. Let the mixture cool slightly.

3 Put the eggs, sugar, and vanilla in a mixing bowl and beat together with an electric handheld mixer until the mixture begins to turn frothy. Stir in the chocolate mixture until combined.

4 Sift the flour and cocoa powder into the bowl and sprinkle with the nuts. Stir together gently, then turn the batter into the pan and level the surface.

5 Bake in the preheated oven for 18–20 minutes, or until the crust feels dry but gives a little when gently pressed. (If you're unsure, it's better to undercook brownies slightly.) Let stand in the pan for 10 minutes, then transfer to a wire rack to cool. Cut the cake into 25 squares.

Cookie Jar

Cookie Jar

Abatch of cookies fresh from the oven is perhaps the surest way to entice company into your kitchen (solitary cooks, be warned). They are also one of the quickest forms of baking, so they are ideal for busy families with a lot of hungry mouths, or for that moment when you just want something butterly sweet and downright comforting.

In one swift movement—taking into account some melting, mixing, and a quick blast in the oven—you have dozens of crisp and chewy treats perfect for friends and family. A foolproof option for bake sales and parties, they can also be stored in a jar to keep you going through the week.

The key items to invest in are a number of solid, flat metal baking sheets that will fit in your oven with space all around for hot air to circulate. Here's a short summary of the other equipment you will need:

Two or three metal baking sheets
Parchment paper
Circular cookie cutter
Pastry bag
Large star tip
Wire cooling racks
Rolling pin
Sharp serrated knife

There are a few tips you can follow to make sure your cookies turn out perfectly every time:

❦ Be sure you read the recipe through before starting and don't skip any stages; if the recipe asks for you to chill the dough, this is because it makes the dough easier to cut.

❦ Preheat the oven to the correct temperature.

❦ Do any chopping, slicing, or grating of ingredients before you start mixing them.

❦ When baking drop cookies, make sure you space them well apart on the baking sheets to allow for expansion.

❦ Bake in the middle of the oven. If you have two sheets, swap them around halfway through the cooking time so the cookies bake evenly.

❦ Freshly baked cookies are soft when they first come out the oven, so let them cool slightly on the baking sheet before transferring to a wire rack to cool completely.

❦ Never store cookies in a container with cake, because they will lose their crispness. Instead, store in a separate airtight container.

Mini Florentines

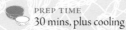

MAKES	PREP TIME	COOK TIME
40	30 mins, plus cooling	20 mins

Ingredients

6 tablespoons butter, plus extra for greasing

flour, for dusting

⅓ cup superfine sugar or granulated sugar

2 tablespoons golden raisins or raisins

2 tablespoons chopped candied cherries

2 tablespoons chopped preserved ginger

3 tablespoons sunflower seeds

1 cup slivered almonds

2 tablespoons heavy cream

6 ounces semisweet or milk chocolate, broken into pieces

Method

1 Preheat the oven to 350°F. Grease and flour two baking sheets or line with wax paper.

2 Put the butter in a small saucepan and heat gently until melted. Add the sugar, stir until dissolved, then bring the mixture to a boil. Remove from the heat and stir in the golden raisins, cherries, ginger, sunflower seeds, and almonds. Mix well, then beat in the cream.

3 Place small teaspoons of the fruit-and-nut mixture onto the prepared baking sheets, allowing plenty of room for the dough to spread during baking. Bake in the preheated oven for 10–12 minutes, or until light golden.

4 Remove from the oven and, while still hot, use a circular cookie cutter to pull in the edges to form perfect circles. Let cool and turn crispy before removing from the baking sheets.

5 Put the chocolate in a heatproof bowl set over a saucepan of simmering water, making sure the bowl doesn't come in contact with the water, and heat until melted. Spread most of the chocolate onto a sheet of wax paper. When the chocolate is on the point of setting, place the cookies, flat-side down, on the chocolate and let it harden completely.

6 Cut around the florentines and remove from the wax paper. Spread a little more chocolate on the coated side of the florentines and use a fork to mark waves in the chocolate. Let stand to set. Keep cool.

Melting Moments

🧁 MAKES
32

🥧 PREP TIME
15 mins

🧤 COOK TIME
15–20 mins

Ingredients

3 sticks unsalted butter, softened

⅔ cup confectioners' sugar

½ teaspoon vanilla extract

2⅓ cups all-purpose flour

⅓ cup cornstarch

Method

1 Preheat the oven to 350°F. Line two large baking sheets with parchment paper.

2 Place the butter and confectioners' sugar in a large bowl and beat together until light and fluffy, then beat in the

vanilla extract. Sift in the flour and cornstarch and mix thoroughly.

3 Spoon the batter into a pastry bag fitted with a large star tip and pipe cookies onto the prepared baking sheets, spaced well apart.

4 Bake in the preheated oven for 15–20 minutes, or until golden brown. Let cool on the baking sheets.

Viennese Cookies

 MAKES
16

 PREP TIME
20 mins, plus cooling

 COOK TIME
20 mins

Ingredients

1 stick unsalted butter,
plus extra for greasing

2 tablespoons superfine sugar
or granulated sugar

½ teaspoon vanilla extract

¾ cup all-purpose flour

¾ teaspoon baking powder

4 ounces semisweet chocolate

Method

1 Preheat the oven to 325°F. Lightly grease two baking sheets.

2 Put the butter, sugar, and vanilla extract in a bowl and cream together until pale and fluffy. Stir in the flour and baking powder, mixing evenly to a fairly stiff batter.

3 Place the batter in a pastry bag fitted with a large star tip and pipe 16 logs, each 2½ inches long, onto the prepared baking sheets spaced well apart.

4 Bake in the preheated oven for 10–15 minutes, until golden brown. Let cool on the baking sheets for a few minutes, then transfer the cookies to wire racks to cool completely.

5 Place the chocolate in a small heatproof bowl set over a saucepan of simmering water, making sure the bowl doesn't come in contact with the water, and heat until melted. Remove the pan from the heat. Dip the ends of each cookie into the chocolate and let set.

Black & White Cookies

🧁 **MAKES**
20

🍮 **PREP TIME**
20 mins, plus chilling

🧤 **COOK TIME**
20 mins

Ingredients

1 stick unsalted butter, softened, plus extra for greasing

1 teaspoon vanilla extract

¾ cup superfine sugar or granulated sugar

2 eggs, beaten

2⅓ cups all-purpose flour

½ teaspoon baking powder

1 cup milk

ICING

1¾ cups confectioners' sugar

½ cup heavy cream

⅛ teaspoon vanilla extract

3 ounces semisweet chocolate, broken into pieces

Method

1 Preheat the oven to 375°F. Grease three baking sheets. Put the butter, vanilla extract, and superfine sugar in a large bowl. Beat the mixture with an electric mixer until light and fluffy, and then beat in the eggs one at a time.

2 Sift the flour and baking powder and fold into the creamed mixture, loosening with milk as you work until both are used up and the batter is of dropping consistency. Drop heaping tablespoons of the batter, spaced well apart, on the prepared baking sheets. Place in the preheated oven and bake for 15 minutes, or until turning golden at the edges and light to the touch. Transfer to wire racks to cool completely.

3 To make the icing, put the confectioners' sugar in a bowl and mix in half the cream and the vanilla extract. The consistency should be thick but spreadable. Using a spatula, spread half of each cookie with white icing. Now, put the chocolate in a bowl set over a saucepan of simmering water, making sure the bowl doesn't come in contact with the water, and heat until melted. Remove from the heat and stir in the remaining cream. Spread the dark icing over the uncoated cookie halves.

1

2

3

Pistachio & Almond Tuiles

MAKES
6

PREP TIME
30 mins, plus cooling

COOK TIME
10–15 mins

Ingredients

1 egg white

¼ cup superfine sugar
or granulated sugar

3 tablespoons all-purpose flour

¼ cup finely chopped
pistachio nuts

¼ cup ground almonds
(almond meal)

½ teaspoon almond extract

3 tablespoons unsalted butter,
melted and cooled

Method

1 Preheat the oven to 325°F. Line two
baking sheets with parchment paper.

2 Whisk the egg white lightly with the
sugar, then stir in the flour, pistachios,
ground almonds, almond extract, and
butter, mixing to a soft batter.

3 Place walnut-size spoonfuls of
the batter on the prepared baking
sheets and use the back of the spoon
to spread as thinly as possible.
Bake in the preheated oven for
10–15 minutes, until pale golden.

4 Quickly lift each cookie with a spatula
and place over the side of a rolling
pin to shape into a curve. When set,
transfer to a wire rack to cool.

Orange & Lemon Cookies

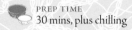

MAKES 30   **PREP TIME** 30 mins, plus chilling   **COOK TIME** 10–15 mins

Ingredients

2 sticks butter, softened

⅔ cup superfine sugar or granulated

1 egg yolk, lightly beaten

2¼ cups all-purpose flour

pinch of salt

finely grated rind of 1 orange

finely grated rind of 1 lemon

TO DECORATE

1 tablespoon lightly beaten egg white

1 tablespoon lemon juice

1 cup confectioners' sugar

few drops yellow food coloring

few drops orange food coloring

about 15 lemon jelly candies

about 15 orange jelly candies

Method

1 Put the butter and sugar into a bowl and mix well with a wooden spoon, then beat in the egg yolk. Sift together the flour and salt into the mixture and stir until thoroughly combined. Halve the dough and gently knead the orange rind into one half and the lemon rind into the other. Shape into balls, wrap in plastic wrap, and chill in the refrigerator for 30–60 minutes.

2 Preheat the oven to 375°F. Line two baking sheets with parchment paper.

3 Unwrap the orange-flavor dough and roll out between two sheets of parchment paper. Stamp out circles with a 2½-inch cutter and put them on a prepared baking sheet spaced well apart. Repeat with the lemon-flavor dough and stamp out crescents. Put them on the other prepared baking sheet spaced well apart.

4 Bake for 10–15 minutes, until golden brown. Let cool for 5–10 minutes, then carefully transfer to wire racks to cool completely.

5 To decorate, mix together the egg white and lemon juice. Gradually beat in the confectioners' sugar with a wooden spoon until smooth. Spoon half the icing into another bowl. Stir yellow food coloring into one bowl and orange into the other. With the cookies on the rack, spread the icing over the cookies and decorate with the jelly candies. Let set.

Blueberry & Orange Cookies

🧁 MAKES
30

🥣 PREP TIME
25 mins, plus chilling

🧤 COOK TIME
10–15 mins

Ingredients

2 sticks butter, softened

⅔ cup superfine sugar
or granulated sugar

1 egg yolk, lightly beaten

1 teaspoon orange extract

2¼ cups all-purpose flour

pinch of salt

¾ cup dried blueberries

½ cup cream cheese

grated rind of 1 orange

⅓ cup finely chopped
macadamia nuts

Method

1 Put the butter and sugar into a bowl and mix well with a wooden spoon, then beat in the egg yolk and orange extract. Sift the flour and salt into the mixture, add the blueberries, and stir until thoroughly combined. Shape the dough into a log, wrap in plastic wrap, and chill in the refrigerator for 30–60 minutes.

2 Preheat the oven to 375°F. Line two baking sheets with parchment paper.

3 Unwrap the dough and cut into ¼-inch slices with a sharp serrated knife. Put them on the prepared baking sheets, spaced well apart.

4 Bake for 10–15 minutes, until golden brown. Let cool on the baking sheets for 5–10 minutes, then using a spatula, carefully transfer to wire racks to cool completely.

5 Just before serving, beat the cream cheese in a bowl and stir in the orange rind. Spread the mixture over the cookies and sprinkle with the chopped nuts.

1

3

5

Pastry Cream Cookies

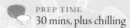

MAKES	PREP TIME	COOK TIME
15	30 mins, plus chilling	20 mins

Ingredients

2 sticks butter, softened

⅔ cup superfine sugar or granulated sugar, plus extra for decoration

1 egg, separated

2 teaspoons vanilla extract

2¼ cups all-purpose flour

pinch of salt

60 red currants or blueberries

1¾ cups confectioners' sugar, sifted

¼ teaspoon lemon extract

PASTRY CREAM

2 egg yolks, lightly beaten

¼ cup superfine sugar or granulated sugar

1 tablespoon cornstarch

1 heaping tablespoon all-purpose flour

1¼ cups milk

few drops of vanilla extract

1 egg white

Method

1 Put the butter and sugar in a large bowl and beat together. Lightly beat the egg yolk and then beat into the mixture with the vanilla extract. Sift in the flour and salt and stir until thoroughly combined. Halve the dough, wrap in plastic wrap, and chill in the refrigerator for 45 minutes.

2 Preheat the oven to 375°F. Line two large baking sheets with parchment paper. Roll out the dough between sheets of parchment paper. Cut out 30 circles with a 2½-inch cookie cutter and place them on the baking sheets. Bake in the preheated oven for 12 minutes, or until golden brown. Let cool for 5 minutes, then transfer to wire racks to cool.

3 To make the pastry cream, beat together the egg yolks and sugar. Sift in the cornstarch and flour and beat well. Stir in 3 tablespoons of the milk and the vanilla extract. Bring the remaining milk to a boil, then whisk it into the mixture. Return to the pan and bring to a boil, stirring, then beat until cool.

4 Whisk the egg white until stiff. Spoon a little pastry cream into a bowl, fold in the egg white, then fold into the rest of the cream. Heat for 2 minutes, then let cool. Sandwich together the cookies with the pastry cream.

5 Beat the egg white. Dip the red currants or blueberries into the beaten egg white and roll in superfine sugar. Mix the confectioners' sugar, lemon extract, and enough water to make a smooth icing. Spread the icing over the cookies and decorate with the berries.

Homemade Gifts

With the growing trend for all things vintage, making your own gifts has never been more popular. Homemade cookies make wonderful gifts—wrapped in cellophane and tied with a bow, they are sure to impress. Add a homemade gift tag and the homemade gift is complete! The gift tags on the opposite page can be photocopied and glued onto cardstock.

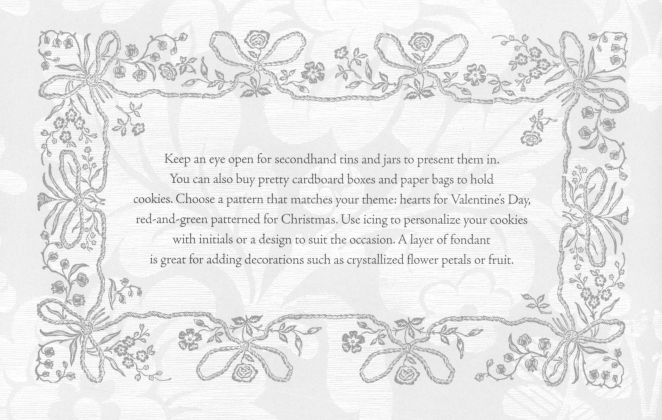

Keep an eye open for secondhand tins and jars to present them in.
You can also buy pretty cardboard boxes and paper bags to hold
cookies. Choose a pattern that matches your theme: hearts for Valentine's Day,
red-and-green patterned for Christmas. Use icing to personalize your cookies
with initials or a design to suit the occasion. A layer of fondant
is great for adding decorations such as crystallized flower petals or fruit.

Baked with love by

....

Created with love by

....

Try these delicious

Date made

Ingredients

Created with love by

....

Created with love by

....

Baked with love by

....

Rose Water Cookies

MAKES 60 | **PREP TIME** 25 mins, plus chilling | **COOK TIME** 10–12 mins

Ingredients

2 sticks butter, softened

1 cup plus 2 tablespoons superfine sugar or granulated sugar

1 extra-large egg, lightly beaten

1 tablespoon rose water

2¼ cups all-purpose flour

1 teaspoon baking powder

pinch of salt

ICING

1 egg white

25 cups confectioners' sugar

2 teaspoons all-purpose flour

2 teaspoons rose water

few drops of pink food coloring

Method

1 Put the butter and sugar in a large bowl and beat together until light and fluffy, then beat in the egg and rose water. Sift together the flour, baking powder, and salt into the mixture and stir until combined. Shape the dough into a log, wrap in plastic wrap, and chill in the refrigerator for 1–2 hours.

2 Preheat the oven to 375°F. Line two to three baking sheets with parchment paper.

3 Unwrap the dough, cut into thin slices with a sharp serrated knife, and place on the baking sheets, spaced well apart.

4 Bake in the preheated oven for 10–12 minutes, or until light golden brown. Let cool on the baking sheets for 10 minutes, then transfer the cookies to wire racks to cool completely.

5 To make the icing, use a fork to beat the egg white lightly in a bowl. Sift in half the confectioners' sugar and stir well, then sift in the remaining confectioners' sugar and flour and mix in enough rose water to make a smooth, easy-to-spread icing. Stir in a few drops of pink food coloring.

6 With the cookies on the racks, gently spread the icing over them and let set.

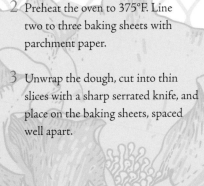

Chocolate Wreaths

 MAKES
16

PREP TIME
15 mins, plus cooling

COOK TIME
15–20 mins

Ingredients

1 stick butter, softened,
plus extra for greasing

⅓ cup confectioners' sugar

1 cup all-purpose flour

3 tablespoons cornstarch

3 tablespoons unsweetened
cocoa powder

½ teaspoon vanilla extract

ICING

¾ cups confectioners' sugar

2 teaspoons unsweetened
cocoa powder

2 tablespoons milk

Method

1 Preheat the oven to 350°F. Grease two
baking sheets.

2 Put the butter and confectioners'
sugar in a bowl and beat together
until pale and creamy. Sift in the flour,
cornstarch, and cocoa powder and
beat well until smooth and creamy.
Beat in the vanilla extract.

3 Spoon the batter into a large pastry
bag fitted with a large star tip and pipe
16 circles, ¾ inch in diameter, onto
the prepared baking sheets.

4 Bake in the preheated oven for
15–20 minutes, until just firm.
Let cool on the baking sheets for
5 minutes, then transfer to a wire
rack to cool completely.

5 To make the icing, sift the
confectioners' sugar and cocoa
powder into a bowl and beat in the
milk to make a smooth icing. Spoon
the icing on top of the cookies.

2

3

5

Perfect Pastries & Pies

Perfect Pastries & Pies

It's incredible to think that the simple alchemy of pastry, made with flour, fat, and water, has the power to revolutionize your home baking. Line a tart pan with a thin layer of sweet pie dough and any fruit or dairy products can quickly be transformed into a delicious pie or tart.

There are, of course, different types of pastry for different requirements. Choux pastry, as used in chocolate éclairs, is a thick cooked blend of flour and butter with eggs beaten through it. Piped and baked, it results in light, airy pastry with a hollow cavity in the center, perfect for filling with luscious pastry cream.

Puff pastry consists of thin layers, which billow into crisp airiness when baked, making it suitable for pastries such as apple turnovers and sweet puffs. The most versatile pastry in this chapter is, however, sweet pie dough. Rolled thinly, it provides a crisp piecrust for everything from Mixed Berry Tarts to decadent Honey, Walnut & Ricotta Pies.

Useful equipment:
Baking sheet
Large pastry bag and plain tip
Pastry brush
12-cup muffin pan and cupcake pan
Rolling pin
Plain and fluted cookie cutters
Individual tart pans (preferably metal)
Parchment paper
Pie weights or dried beans

Cinnamon Swirls

🧁 **MAKES**
12

🥣 **PREP TIME**
1 hour, plus rising

🧤 **COOK TIME**
20–30 mins

Ingredients

1⅓ cups white bread flour

½ teaspoon salt

2¼ teaspoons active dry yeast

2 tablespoons butter, cut into small pieces, plus extra for greasing

1 egg, lightly beaten

½ cup lukewarm milk

2 tablespoons maple syrup, for glazing

FILLING

4 tablespoons butter, softened

2 teaspoons ground cinnamon

¼ cup firmly packed light brown sugar

⅓ cup dried currants

Method

1 Grease a baking sheet with a little butter.

2 Sift the flour and salt into a mixing bowl. Stir in the yeast. Rub in the butter with your fingertips until the mixture resembles bread crumbs. Add the egg and milk and mix to form a dough.

3 Form the dough into a ball, place in a greased bowl, cover with plastic wrap, and let stand in a warm place for

about 40 minutes, or until doubled in size. Knead the dough for 1 minute, then roll out to a rectangle measuring 12 x 9 inches.

4 To make the filling, cream together the butter, cinnamon, and sugar until light and fluffy. Spread the filling evenly over the dough rectangle, leaving a 1-inch border all around. Sprinkle the currants evenly over the top.

5 Roll up the dough from one of the long edges, and press down to seal. Cut the roll into 12 slices. Place them, cut-side down, on the baking sheet, cover, and let stand for 30 minutes.

6 Meanwhile, preheat the oven to 375°F. Bake the cinnamon swirls in the preheated oven for 20–30 minutes, or until well-risen. Brush with the maple syrup and let cool slightly before serving.

Apple Turnovers

MAKES
8

PREP TIME
40 mins plus cooling

COOK TIME
15–20 mins

Ingredients

1 sheet ready-to-bake
puff pastry

flour, for dusting

milk, for glazing

heavy cream, whipped, to serve

FILLING

3 Granny Smith apples, peeled,
cored, and chopped

grated rind of 1 lemon (optional)

pinch of ground cloves (optional)

3 tablespoons sugar

ORANGE SUGAR

1 tablespoon sugar, for sprinkling

finely grated rind of 1 orange

Method

1 To make the filling, mix together the apples, lemon rind, and ground cloves, if using, but do not add the sugar yet, or the juice will seep out of the apples. For the orange sugar, mix together the sugar and orange rind.

2 Preheat the oven to 425°F. Roll out the puff pastry on a floured work surface into a 24 x 12-inch rectangle. Cut the

pastry in half lengthwise, then across into four to make eight 6-inch squares.

3 Mix the sugar into the apple filling. Brush each square lightly with milk and place a little of the apple filling in the center. Fold over one corner diagonally to meet the opposite one, making a triangular turnover, and press the edges together firmly.

Place on a baking sheet. Repeat with the remaining squares. Brush with milk and sprinkle with the orange sugar. Bake in the preheated oven for 15–20 minutes, or until browned. Let cool on a wire rack. Serve with the heavy cream.

1

2

3

Chocolate Éclairs

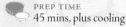

 MAKES
12

PREP TIME
45 mins, plus cooling

COOK TIME
45 mins

Ingredients

CHOUX PASTRY

⅔ cup water

5 tablespoons butter,
cut into small pieces,
plus extra for greasing

¾ cup all-purpose flour, sifted

2 eggs

PASTRY CREAM

2 eggs, lightly beaten

¼ cup superfine sugar

2 tablespoons cornstarch

1¼ cups milk

½ teaspoon vanilla extract

FROSTING

2 tablespoons butter

1 tablespoon milk

1 tablespoon unsweetened
cocoa powder

½ cup confectioners' sugar

2 ounces milk chocolate

Method

1 Preheat the oven to 400°F. Lightly grease a baking sheet.

2 To make the choux pastry, put the water in a saucepan, add the butter and heat gently until the butter melts. Bring to a rolling boil, then remove the saucepan from the heat and add the flour all at once, beating well until the mixture leaves the sides of the saucepan and forms a ball. Let cool slightly, then gradually beat in the eggs to form a smooth, glossy mixture. Spoon into a large pastry bag fitted with a ½-inch plain tip.

3 Sprinkle the baking sheet with a little water. Pipe 12 éclairs, 3 inches long, spaced well apart. Bake for 30–35 minutes, or until crisp and golden. Make a small slit in the side of each éclair to let the steam escape. Let cool on a wire rack.

4 Meanwhile, make the pastry cream. Whisk the eggs and sugar until thick and creamy, then fold in the cornstarch. Heat the milk until almost boiling and pour onto the eggs, whisking. Transfer to the saucepan and cook over low heat, stirring until thick. Remove the pan from the heat and stir in the vanilla extract. Cover with parchment paper and let cool.

5 To make the frosting, melt the butter with the milk in a saucepan. Remove from the heat and stir in the cocoa and sugar. Split the éclairs lengthwise and pipe in the pastry cream. Spread the frosting over the top of the éclairs. Break up the milk chocolate into pieces and place in a heatproof bowl set over a saucepan of simmering water, making sure the bowl doesn't come in contact with the water, and heat until melted. Drizzle over the chocolate frosting and let set. Serve immediately.

Caramelized Apple Tarts

 MAKES
12

PREP TIME
45 mins, plus chilling

COOK TIME
36 mins

Ingredients

1 (15-ounce) package rolled dough piecrust, chilled

a little all-purpose flour, for dusting

5 Granny Smith apples, quartered, cored, and peeled

⅓ cup superfine sugar or granulated sugar

finely grated rind and juice of 1 lemon

2 eggs

1 tablespoon butter, plus extra for greasing

3 tablespoons confectioners' sugar, sifted

Method

1 Lightly grease a 12-cup muffin pan. Roll the dough out thinly on a lightly floured surface. Using a plain cookie cutter, stamp out 12 circles, each 4 inches in diameter. Press these gently into the prepared pan, rerolling the trimmings as needed. Prick the bottom of each with a fork, then chill in the refrigerator for 15 minutes.

2 Preheat the oven to 375°F. Line the pastry shells with squares of crumpled parchment paper and pie weights or dried beans. Bake in the preheated oven for 10 minutes. Remove the paper and beans and cook the shells for an additional 2–3 minutes, or until the bottom of the pastry is crisp and dry. Reduce the oven temperature to 350°F.

3 Coarsely grate eight of the apple quarters into a mixing bowl. Add two-thirds of the superfine sugar, all the lemon rind and juice, and the eggs and beat together. Spoon the filling into the pastry shells.

4 Thinly slice the remaining apples and arrange them overlapping on top of the pies. Sprinkle with the remaining superfine sugar and then dot the pies with the butter. Bake in the preheated oven for 20–25 minutes, or until the filling is set.

5 Dust with the confectioners' sugar and return the pies to the oven for 5 minutes, or until the sugar has caramelized pale gold. Let cool in the pan for 10 minutes, then transfer the tarts to a wire rack to cool. Serve warm or cold.

Blueberry Tarts

Ingredients

2 cups blueberries

2 teaspoons cornstarch

¼ cup superfine sugar
or granulated sugar

4 teaspoons water

½ cup all-purpose flour,
plus extra for dusting

grated rind of 1 lemon

3 tablespoons butter, diced,
plus extra for greasing

1 (15-ounce) package rolled
dough pie crust, chilled

Method

1 Preheat the oven to 375°F. Lightly grease two mini 12-cup cupcake pans.

2 Put half the blueberries in a small saucepan with the cornstarch, half the superfine sugar, and all the water. Cook over medium heat, stirring continuously, for 2–3 minutes. Take the pan off the heat and add the remaining blueberries.

3 For the streusel, put the flour, lemon rind, butter, and remaining sugar in a bowl. Toss together, then rub it through your fingers and thumbs until it looks like fine bread crumbs.

4 Roll the dough out thinly on a lightly floured surface. Using a fluted cookie cutter, stamp out 24 circles each 2½ inches in diameter. Press these into the prepared pans, rerolling trimmings as needed. Spoon the blueberry filling into the shells, then sprinkle the tops of the tarts with the streusel mixture. Bake in the preheated oven for 15 minutes, or until the topping is pale gold. Leave to cool in the pans for 10 minutes, then loosen with a round-bladed knife and transfer to a wire rack to cool.

Mixed Berry Tarts

 MAKES
12

 PREP TIME
25 mins, plus chilling

 COOK TIME
18 mins

Ingredients

1⅔ cups all-purpose flour, plus extra for dusting

⅔ cup confectioners' sugar, sifted

½ cup ground almonds (almond meal)

1 stick butter, plus extra for greasing

1 egg yolk

1 tablespoon milk

fresh mixed berries, to decorate

FILLING

1 cup cream cheese

confectioners' sugar, to taste, plus extra, sifted, for dusting

Method

1 Lightly grease 12 individual tart pans. Sift the flour and confectioners' sugar into a bowl. Stir in the almonds. Add the butter, rubbing in until the mixture resembles bread crumbs. Add the egg yolk and milk and work in until the dough binds together. Wrap in plastic wrap and chill for 30 minutes. Meanwhile, preheat the oven to 400°F.

2 Roll out the dough on a lightly floured surface and use to line the tart pans. Prick the bottoms and press a piece of aluminum foil into each.

3 Bake in the preheated oven for 10–15 minutes, or until light golden brown. Remove the foil and bake for an additional 2–3 minutes. Transfer to a wire rack to cool.

4 To make the filling, put the cream cheese and confectioners' sugar in a bowl and mix together. Put a spoonful of filling in each tart and arrange the berries on top.

5 Dust with sifted confectioners' sugar and serve.

93

Salted Caramel Pies

MAKES
4

PREP TIME
30 mins, plus chilling

COOK TIME
10 mins

Ingredients

CRUMB CRUST

1½ cups finely crushed
graham crackers

6 tablespoons butter, melted

FILLING

1½ cups superfine sugar or
granulated sugar

1¼ sticks butter

¼ teaspoon sea salt crystals

½ cup heavy cream

TOPPING

⅔ cup heavy cream

chocolate curls or shavings

Method

1 To make the crumb crust, put the crushed cookies in a bowl and stir in the melted butter. Divide the mixture among four individual tart pans and press down firmly into the bottom and up the sides of each pan. Chill in the refrigerator for 30 minutes.

2 To make the filling, put the sugar and ¼ cup of water into a heavy saucepan. Heat gently, stirring, until the sugar has dissolved. Bring the syrup to a boil and boil, without stirring, until the liquid is a golden color. Remove from the heat and cool for 2 minutes, then carefully stir in the butter and half the salt.

3 Gradually whisk in the cream and continue whisking until the mixture is smooth and glossy. Transfer to a heatproof bowl and let cool and thicken, stirring occasionally. Stir in the rest of the salt. Spoon the cooled caramel into the tart crusts.

4 For the topping, whip the cream until it holds soft peaks. Drop large spoonfuls on top of the caramel filling, sprinkle with the chocolate curls or shavings, and serve.

1

2

3

Pies for Parties

The trend toward baking individual or miniature tarts is, let's face it, a great way of having your own dessert and eating it all by yourself. Mini pies are easier to serve at parties, preventing the headache of baking one huge pie and hoping everyone gets an equal slice. Simple decorations, such as chocolate curls, a little streusel topping, a sprinkling of confectioners' sugar, or a spoonful of whipped cream, add a finishing touch. Or, if you really want to get your *pâtissière* hat on, whip a pastry bag out and go for it.

When it comes to serving your miniature pastries, help guests and friends by providing the right cutlery. Something creamy with a soft filling, such as berries, or caramelized apple tart will require a dessert fork. Pastries, such as apple turnovers or upside-down apple tart, are at their best warm, served on a plate with a dollop of cream and a spoon, while a small puff or tart can be eaten with fingers—but be sure to provide napkins.

Caramel Chocolate Puffs

MAKES
12

PREP TIME
30 mins, plus chilling

COOK TIME
20–25 mins

Ingredients

1 (18-ounce) package
ready-to-bake puff pastry

5 ounces semisweet chocolate,
broken into pieces

1¼ cups heavy cream

¼ cup superfine sugar or
granulated sugar

4 egg yolks

¼ cup store-bought caramel sauce

whipped cream, to serve

unsweetened cocoa powder,
for dusting

Method

1 Line the bottoms of a 12-cup muffin pan with circles of parchment paper. Cut out twelve 2-inch circles from the edge of the pastry and cut the remainder into 12 strips. Roll the strips to half their thickness and line the sides of each hole with a strip. Place a circle of pastry in each bottom and press together to seal and make a tart shell. Prick the bottoms and chill in the refrigerator for 30 minutes.

2 Preheat the oven to 400°F. While the pastry is chilling, put the chocolate in a heatproof bowl set over a saucepan of simmering water, making sure the bowl doesn't come in contact with the water, and heat until melted. Let cool slightly, then stir in the cream.

3 Put the sugar and egg yolks in a bowl and beat together, then mix well with the melted chocolate. Put a teaspoonful of the caramel sauce

into each tart shell, then divide the chocolate mixture evenly among the tarts. Bake in the preheated oven for 20–25 minutes, turning the pan around halfway through cooking, until just set. Let cool in the pan, then remove carefully and serve with whipped cream, dusted with cocoa.

Honey, Walnut & Ricotta Pies

MAKES
24

PREP TIME
45 mins, plus cooling

COOK TIME
25 mins

Ingredients

a little butter, for greasing

a little olive oil, for greasing

1 sheet rolled dough
piecrust, chilled

a little all-purpose flour,
for dusting

1 cup walnut pieces

1 cup ricotta cheese

2 egg yolks

⅓ cup orange-blossom honey

a large pinch of ground cinnamon

½ cup granulated sugar

1 tablespoon water

1 cup Greek yogurt,
to serve

Method

1 Lightly grease two mini 12-cup cupcake pans and oil a baking sheet. Preheat the oven to 350°F.

2 Roll the dough out thinly on a lightly floured surface. Using a fluted cookie cutter, stamp out 24 circles, each 2½ inches in diameter. Press these gently into the prepared pans, rerolling the trimmings as needed.

3 Lightly toast half the walnut pieces in a dry, nonstick skillet. Let them cool, then coarsely chop them.

4 Lightly beat together the ricotta, egg yolks, ¼ cup of the honey, and the cinnamon in a mixing bowl until just mixed. Stir in the toasted walnuts. Spoon the filling into the shells.

5 Bake in the preheated oven for 20 minutes, or until the filling is golden brown. Let stand in the pans for 10 minutes to cool.

6 Meanwhile, for the praline, put the sugar, remaining 1 tablespoon of honey, and the water into the skillet and heat gently without stirring until the sugar has dissolved. Tilt the skillet to mix any remaining grains of sugar into the syrup. Add the remaining walnuts and cook over medium heat, again without stirring, for about 5 minutes, or until the syrup turns a rich golden brown. Keep a watchful eye on the syrup, because it will suddenly begin to change color, darkening first around the edges. Tilt the skillet to mix if needed, then

quickly pour the praline onto the prepared baking sheet and let cool and harden.

7 Loosen the pies with a blunt knife and transfer them to a plate. Just before serving, top them with spoonfuls of yogurt. Loosen the praline from the baking sheet with a knife, then break or cut it into thin shards and press pieces of it into the yogurt.

Upside-down Apple Tart

🧁 SERVES
6

🥣 PREP TIME
20 mins, plus resting

🧤 COOK TIME
45 mins

Ingredients

*1 cup superfine sugar or
granulated sugar*

1¼ sticks unsalted butter

*7 Pippin or Golden Delicious
apples (about 1¾ pounds)*

*1½ sheets ready-to-bake
puff pastry*

Method

1 Place an 8-inch ovenproof skillet over low heat and add the sugar. Melt the sugar until it starts to caramelize, but do not let it burn, then add the butter and stir it in to make a light toffee sauce. Remove from the heat.

2 Peel the apples and cut them into eighths vertically. Core the apples and lay them in the skillet on top of the toffee sauce, cut-side up. They should fill the skillet. If there are any large gaps, add a few more apple pieces. Put the skillet over medium heat and cover. Simmer, without stirring, for about 5–10 minutes, until the apples have soaked up some of the sauce, then remove from the heat.

3 Preheat the oven to 375°F. Roll out the pastry so that it will thickly cover the skillet, with extra overhanging the sides. Lay it on top of the apples and tuck the edges down inside between the fruit and the skillet until it is sealed. Don't worry about making it look too neat—it will be turned over before serving.

4 Put the skillet into the preheated oven and bake for 25–35 minutes, checking to make sure the pastry doesn't burn. The pastry should be puffed and golden. Remove from the oven and let rest for 30–60 minutes.

5 To serve, make sure the tart is still a little warm and place a plate on top of the skillet. Carefully turn it over and lift the skillet off. Serve warm.

Special Moments

Special Moments

For every special day and holiday, tradition dictates that there will be cake. Whether it's a stand of birthday cupcakes, each with a candle, wedding cake festooned in iced rosebuds, or a plateful of Easter cookies, you can always tell an occasion from a dessert.

When planning your party, try following these few simple rules: plan as far in advance as possible, preparing and freezing what food you can; consider the tastes of your guests; provide enough food, drink, and chairs; and ask for help if you need it. Oh, and don't be afraid to exercise your imagination.

Party planning checklist:

* Draw up invitation list
* Choose theme; make, borrow, or buy decorations and props
* Send invitations
* Design menu; plan what to make in advance and write a shopping list
* Clean and prepare linen and cutlery
* Plan what dishes you will need; source whatever you don't have
* Decorate for the occasion
* Buy and arrange flowers; decorate the house the day before
* On the day; arrange chairs, lay the table, and make last-minute touches to food

Photocopy this invitation and send out to your guests.

Invitation

Dear ....

You have been invited to ....

....

By ....

On ....

At ....

RSVP by ....

Summer Flower Cupcakes

 MAKES
8

 PREP TIME
45 mins, plus cooling

 COOK TIME
15–20 mins

Ingredients

1 stick butter, softened,
or soft margarine

½ cup superfine sugar or
granulated sugar

2 teaspoons rose water

2 extra-large eggs,
lightly beaten

1 cup all-purpose flour

1 teaspoon baking powder

TO DECORATE

4 ounces pink
ready-to-use fondant

3 ounces white

ready-to-use fondant

3 ounces blue
ready-to-use fondant

tube of yellow writing icing

1½ sticks unsalted butter,
softened

⅓ cup heavy cream

2¾ cups confectioners' sugar,
plus extra for dusting

green food coloring

Method

1 Preheat the oven to 350°F. Line a
12-cup muffin pan with 8 paper liners.

2 Put the butter, superfine sugar,
and rose water in a large bowl and
beat together until light and fluffy.
Gradually beat in the eggs. Sift in
the flour and baking powder and,
using a metal spoon, fold in gently.

3 Spoon the batter into the paper
liners. Bake in the preheated oven for
15–20 minutes, or until risen, golden
and firm to the touch. Transfer to a
wire rack and let cool.

4 To decorate, roll out the pink fondant
to a thickness of ¼ inch on a surface
lightly dusted with confectioners'
sugar. Using a small butterfly cutter,
stamp out 16 butterflies. Roll out the
white and blue fondants to the same
thickness and, using a small daisy
cutter, stamp out about 40 flowers,
rerolling the fondant as necessary.
Use the yellow writing icing to pipe
centers in the flowers.

5 Put the butter in a bowl and
beat with an electric mixer for
2–3 minutes, until pale and creamy.
Beat in the cream, then gradually
sift in the confectioners' sugar and
continue beating for 2–3 minutes,
until the buttercream is light and
fluffy. Beat in a little green food
coloring to create a light green color.

6 Spoon the buttercream into a
large pastry bag fitted with a
large star tip. Pipe swirls of
buttercream on top of each
cupcake. Decorate with the
fondant butterflies and flowers.

Chocolate Mint Cake Pops

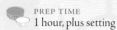

Ingredients

10 ounces semisweet chocolate, coarsely chopped

2 tablespoons unsalted butter, softened

2 ounces hard, mint candies

1 pound milk chocolate

1 cup coarsely chopped miniature marshmallows

28 lollipop sticks

chocolate sprinkles, to decorate

Method

1 Line a baking sheet with parchment paper. Put the semisweet chocolate in a heatproof bowl, set the bowl over a saucepan of gently simmering water, and heat until melted. Stir in the butter. Let stand until the mixture is cool but not beginning to set.

2 Put the mint candies in a plastic food bag and tap firmly with a rolling pin until they are broken into tiny pieces. Finely chop one-sixth of the milk chocolate, then stir it into the melted semisweet chocolate with the mint candies and marshmallows until thoroughly mixed.

3 As soon as the mixture is firm enough to hold its shape, roll it into 28 even balls. Place them on the baking sheet and chill for 30–60 minutes, until firm but not brittle. Push a lollipop stick into each cake pop, then chill for 10 minutes.

4 Coarsely chop the remaining milk chocolate and melt as above, then remove from the heat. Dip a cake pop into the chocolate, turning it until coated. Lift it from the bowl, letting the excess drip back into the bowl, and place it in a cup or glass. Sprinkle with chocolate sprinkles. Repeat

with the remaining cake pops. Chill or let stand in a cool place until the chocolate has set.

Birthday Party Cupcakes

🧁 MAKES
24

 PREP TIME
40 mins, plus cooling

🧤 COOK TIME
15–20 mins

Ingredients

1 cup soft margarine

1 cup superfine sugar or granulated sugar

4 eggs

1¾ cups all-purpose flour, sifted

1¾ teaspoons baking powder

a variety of small candies and chocolates, sugar-coated chocolates, candied fruit, edible sugar flower shapes, sprinkles, and sugar strands

candles and candleholders (optional)

FROSTING

1½ sticks butter, softened

2¾ cups confectioners' sugar

Method

1 Preheat the oven to 350°F. Line two 12-cup cupcake pans with 24 paper liners.

2 Put the margarine, sugar, eggs, flour, and baking powder in a large bowl and, using an electric handheld mixer, beat together until just smooth. Spoon the batter into the paper liners.

3 Bake the cupcakes in the preheated oven for 15–20 minutes, or until well-risen, golden, and firm to the touch. Transfer to a wire rack and let cool.

4 To make the frosting, put the butter in a bowl and beat until fluffy. Sift in the confectioners' sugar and beat together until smooth and creamy. Spoon the frosting into a pastry bag fitted with a large star tip. When the cupcakes are cold, pipe circles of frosting on top of each cupcake, then decorate as you choose. If desired, place a candle in the top of each.

Be My Valentine Whoopie Pies

🧁 MAKES
14

🥣 PREP TIME
20 mins, plus cooling

🧤 COOK TIME
35 mins

Ingredients

2 cups all-purpose flour

1 teaspoon baking soda

large pinch of salt

1 stick butter, softened

¾ cup superfine sugar or granulated sugar

1 extra-large egg, beaten

1 teaspoon vanilla extract

⅔ cup buttermilk

¼ teaspoon edible red liquid food coloring

2 tablespoons pink heart-shaped sugar sprinkles

BUTTERCREAM

1¼ sticks unsalted butter, softened

1 teaspoon vanilla extract

¼ cup heavy cream

2¼ cups confectioners' sugar, sifted

ICING

1¼ cups confectioners' sugar

1–2 tablespoons warm water

few drops edible red liquid food coloring

Method

1 Preheat the oven to 350°F. Line two to three large baking sheets with wax paper. Sift together the all-purpose flour, baking soda, and salt.

2 Put the butter and sugar in a large bowl and beat with an electric handheld mixer until pale and fluffy. Beat in the egg and vanilla extract, followed by half of the flour mixture, then the buttermilk and food coloring. Stir in the rest of the flour mixture and mix until thoroughly incorporated.

3 Pipe or spoon 28 mounds of the batter onto the prepared baking sheets, spaced well apart to allow for spreading. Bake in the preheated oven, one sheet at a time, for 9–11 minutes until risen and just firm to the touch. Cool for 5 minutes, then using a spatula, transfer to a wire rack and let cool completely.

4 For the buttercream, put the butter and vanilla extract in a bowl and beat with an electric handheld mixer for 2–3 minutes, until pale and creamy. Beat in the cream, then gradually beat in the confectioners' sugar and continue beating for 2–3 minutes.

5 For the icing, sift the confectioners' sugar into a bowl and stir in enough water to make a smooth icing that is thick enough to coat the back of a wooden spoon. Beat in a few drops of food coloring to create a pale-pink color.

6 To assemble, spread or pipe the buttercream on the flat side of half of the cakes. Top with the rest of the cakes. Spoon the icing over the whoopie pies and decorate with the heart-shaped sugar sprinkles. Let set.

Traditional Easter Cookies

〰️

🧁 **MAKES**
30

🥣 **PREP TIME**
20 mins, plus cooling

🧤 **COOK TIME**
15 mins

Ingredients

2 sticks butter, softened

¾ cup superfine sugar or granulated sugar, plus extra for sprinkling

1 egg yolk, lightly beaten

2¼ cups all-purpose flour

1 teaspoon allspice

pinch of salt

1 tablespoon candied peel

⅓ cup dried currants

1 egg white, lightly beaten

Method

1 Put the butter and sugar in a large bowl and beat together until light and fluffy, then beat in the egg yolk. Sift together the flour, allspice, and salt into the mixture, add the candied peel and currants, and stir until thoroughly combined. Halve the dough, shape into balls, wrap in plastic wrap, and chill in the refrigerator for 30–60 minutes.

2 Preheat the oven to 375°F. Line three large baking sheets with parchment paper.

3 Unwrap the dough and roll out between two sheets of parchment paper. Cut out cookies with a 2½-inch fluted round cutter and place them on the baking sheets, spaced well apart. Bake in the preheated oven for 7 minutes, then brush with the egg white and sprinkle with the sugar. Bake for an additional 5–8 minutes, or until light golden brown. Let cool on the baking sheets for 5–10 minutes, then transfer to wire racks to cool completely.

Anniversary Cupcakes

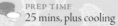

MAKES	PREP TIME	COOK TIME
24	25 mins, plus cooling	15–20 mins

Ingredients

2 sticks butter, softened

1 cup superfine sugar or granulated sugar

1 teaspoon vanilla extract

4 extra-large eggs, lightly beaten

1¾ cups all-purpose flour, sifted

1¾ teaspoons baking powder

⅓ cup milk

FROSTING

1½ sticks unsalted butter

2¾ cups confectioners' sugar

silver or gold candied balls, to decorate

Method

1 Preheat the oven to 350°F. Line two 12-hole cupcake pans with 24 paper liners.

2 Put the butter, sugar, and vanilla extract in a bowl and beat together until light and fluffy. Gradually add the eggs, beating well after each addition. Add the flour and baking powder, and use a large metal spoon to fold into the mixture with the milk. Spoon the batter into the paper liners.

3 Bake the cupcakes in the preheated oven for 15–20 minutes, or until well-risen and firm to the touch. Transfer to a wire rack and let cool.

4 To make the frosting, put the butter in a bowl and beat until fluffy. Sift in the confectioners' sugar and beat together. Put the frosting in a pastry bag, fitted with a star-shaped tip.

5 When the cupcakes are cold, pipe circles of frosting on top of each cupcake. Sprinkle over the silver or gold candied balls before serving.

118

Wedding Day Cupcakes

 MAKES
12

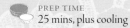 PREP TIME
25 mins, plus cooling

 COOK TIME
15–20 mins

Ingredients

1 stick butter, softened

½ cup superfine sugar or granulated sugar

2 eggs, lightly beaten

1¼ cups all-purpose flour, sifted

1¼ teaspoons baking powder

½ teaspoon vanilla extract

1–2 tablespoons milk

TOPPING

confectioners' sugar, for dusting

8 ounces white ready-to-use fondant

3 tablespoons honey, warmed

2–3 drops pink food coloring

tube of green writing icing

Method

1 Preheat the oven to 400°F. Line a 12-cup cupcake pan with 12 paper liners. Put the butter and superfine sugar into a bowl and beat together until pale and creamy. Gradually add the eggs and continue beating. Fold in the flour and baking powder using a metal spoon. Stir in the vanilla extract and milk.

2 Spoon the batter into the paper liners. Bake in the preheated oven for 15–20 minutes, or until well-risen and firm to the touch. Transfer to a wire rack and let cool.

3 Dust the work surface with confectioners' sugar. Roll out all but one-eighth of the fondant to 8 x 11 inches. Use a cookie cutter to stamp out 12 circles. Brush the cake tops with honey and stick on the circles.

4 To make the rosebuds, knead the remaining fondant with the food coloring. Roll out 12 strips of fondant to ½ x 2½ inches. Roll up and stick on top with honey. Draw on a stem with the writing icing. Let set.

Party Ideas

For a smaller party, set a place at the table for each person, but for a larger party, go for a buffet style, arranging a sideboard with party food. Batches of smaller cakes are perfect for larger gatherings, allowing people to eat with their fingers.

Search online for suppliers of linen, china, and cutlery that will deliver to you. Consider thrift shops and flea markets, too. Dress the table using flowers suitable for the occasion—dusty pink roses and hydrangeas for a "tea party" or bright delphiniums and snapdragons in different-sized pitchers and vases for a summer party.

Tie napkins with ribbon matched to your floral arrangement, add place-cards clipped to wine or champagne glasses and set tea-light candles in jars. For a formal affair, set the table with your best linen, put tapering candles into candelabra, and look for unique items, such as old-fashioned serving bowls. Layered cake stands lend height and a sense of occasion.

Most important, remember to have fun and add the touches that you, personally, love. If you've put a little of yourself into the planning, your guests won't fail to be charmed.

Halloween Mud Pie

SERVES
8

PREP TIME
30 mins, plus cooling

COOK TIME
40 mins

Ingredients

3 ounces semisweet chocolate

6 tablespoons unsalted butter

⅓ cup packed light brown sugar

2 eggs, beaten

½ cup light cream

1 teaspoon vanilla extract

PIE DOUGH

1⅓ cups all-purpose flour, plus extra for dusting

¼ cup unsweetened cocoa powder

⅓ cup packed light brown sugar

6 tablespoons unsalted butter

2–3 tablespoons cold water

TOPPING

1 cup heavy whipping cream

3 ounces semisweet chocolate

Method

1 Preheat the oven to 400°F. To make the dough, sift the flour and cocoa powder into a bowl and stir in the sugar. Rub in the butter with your fingertips until the mixture resembles fine bread crumbs. Add just enough water to bind to a dough.

2 Roll out the dough on a lightly floured work surface to a circle large enough to line a 1¼-inch deep, 8-inch tart pan. Use the dough to line the pan. Prick the bottom with a fork, cover with a piece of waxed paper, and fill with pie weights or dried beans, then bake the shell in the preheated oven for 10 minutes. Remove from the oven and take out the paper and weights. Reduce the oven temperature to 350°F.

3 Put the chocolate and butter into a saucepan and heat over low heat, stirring, until melted. Put the sugar and eggs into a bowl and beat together until smooth, then stir in the chocolate mixture, cream, and vanilla extract.

4 Pour the chocolate mixture into the pastry shell and bake in the oven for 20–25 minutes, or until just set. Let cool.

5 To make the topping, whip the cream until it just holds its shape, then spread over the pie. Melt the chocolate in a bowl set over a saucepan of simmering water, making sure the bowl doesn't come in contact with the water, then spoon into a pastry bag and pipe decorations over the cream. Serve cold.

Christmas Macarons

 MAKES
16

 PREP TIME
30 mins, plus standing

 COOK TIME
10–15 mins

Ingredients

¾ cup ground almonds
(almond meal)

1 cup confectioners' sugar

1 teaspoon ground allspice

2 extra-large egg whites

¼ cup superfine sugar or
granulated sugar

½ teaspoon freshly grated nutmeg

1 teaspoon gold sugar balls

FILLING

4 tablespoons unsalted
butter, softened

juice and finely grated rind of
½ orange

1 teaspoon ground allspice

1 cup confectioners' sugar, sifted

2 tablespoons finely chopped
candied cherries

Method

1 Put the ground almonds,
confectioners' sugar, and allspice
in a food processor and process for
15 seconds. Sift the mixture into
a bowl. Line two baking sheets
with wax paper.

2 Put the egg whites in a large bowl
and whisk until they hold soft peaks.
Gradually whisk in the superfine sugar
to make a firm, glossy meringue. Using
a spatula, fold the almond mixture
into the meringue one-third at a time.
When all the dry ingredients are
thoroughly incorporated, continue
to cut and fold the mixture until it
forms a shiny batter with a thick,
ribbonlike consistency.

3 Pour the batter into a pastry bag
fitted with a ½-inch plain tip. Pipe
32 small circles onto the prepared
baking sheets. Tap the baking
sheets firmly onto a work surface to
remove air bubbles. Sprinkle half the
macarons with the grated nutmeg
and gold sugar balls. Let stand at
room temperature for 30 minutes.
Meanwhile, preheat the oven to 325°F.

4 Bake in the preheated oven for
10–15 minutes. Cool for 10 minutes,
then carefully peel the macarons off
the wax paper. Let cool completely.

5 To make the filling, beat the butter
and orange juice and rind in a bowl
until fluffy. Gradually beat in the
allspice and confectioners' sugar until
smooth and creamy. Fold in the
candied cherries. Use to sandwich
together pairs of macarons.